MONKEYS

Baboons

Mae Woods
ABDO & Daughters

visit us at
www.abdopub.com

Published by Abdo & Daughters, 4940 Viking Drive, Suite 622, Edina, Minnesota 55435.

Copyright © 1998 by Abdo Consulting Group, Inc., Pentagon Tower, P.O. Box 36036, Minneapolis, Minnesota 55435 USA. International copyrights reserved in all countries. No part of this book may be reproduced in any form without written permission from the publisher.

Printed in the United States.

Cover Photo credits: Peter Arnold, Inc.
Interior Photo credits: Peter Arnold, Inc.

Edited by Lori Kinstad Pupeza

Library of Congress Cataloging-in-Publication Data

Woods, Mae.
     Baboons / Mae Woods.
     p. cm. -- (Monkeys)
     Includes index.
     Summary: Describes the physical characteristics, life cycle, social interactions, and different kinds of baboons.
     ISBN 1-56239-596-3
     1. Baboons--Juvenile literature. [1. Baboons.] I. Title. II. Series: Woods, Mae. Monkeys.
     QL737.P93W66   1998
     599.8'2--dc20
                               96-10483
                               CIP
                               AC

Contents

Baboons and Other Monkeys

The name baboon comes from a French word for lip. These monkeys always smack their lips when they greet each other.

Baboons are the largest animals in the monkey family. They are as big as many kinds of **apes**. Like apes, all monkeys are **primates**. One of the main differences between apes and monkeys is that monkeys have tails. Apes and monkeys live for 35 to 40 years.

Monkeys are divided into two types: Old World Monkeys, which live in Africa or Asia, and New World Monkeys. These live in Central or South America. Baboons are Old World Monkeys.

A Gelada baboon from Ethiopia, Africa.

What They Are Like

Baboons are the most unusual looking of all the monkeys. They look more like dogs than other monkeys. Their bodies are covered with thick fur, and they have tails. They have large heads with long **muzzles**. Their small eyes and low brows make them look very **fierce**. This ridged brow protects their eyes from the sun. Baboons have better eyesight than other **primates**.

Their face is hairless and may be black, pink, or multi-colored. It is framed by **ruffs** of fur around the cheeks. Baboons have pouches in their cheeks. They can store food in these pouches to soften it before eating.

There are pads of colored flesh on their backside. These two pads are like cushions. A baboon is able to balance sitting on a rock or the branch of a tree.

A Hamadryas baboon seated on a rock, howling.

How They Live

Baboons use their hands much like humans do. Their arms are slightly longer than their legs. Baboons can stand on their feet, but they walk on all fours and spend most of the day on the ground. At night they climb into the trees. They sleep sitting up with their toes curled around a branch.

Baboons live in a family group. Each group has one father but may have many mothers and babies. Male baboons weigh between 70 and 100 pounds (31 and 45 kg). Females weigh about 35 pounds (15 kg). They have smaller teeth and less hair than male baboons. When they are seated, baboons are over two feet tall.

Opposite page: A Hamadryas baboon moving on all fours.

Different Kinds of Baboons

Baboons live in many areas of Africa and Saudi Arabia. There are four **species** of these monkeys. Each group is different in size, shape, and color.

The **mandrill** is the most colorful baboon. The male's face looks like it has paint on it. He has a bright red nose with blue ridges around it. His beard is yellow, and he has a white band around the back of his neck. His sitting pads are purple and red. Mandrills live in the forests of west Africa.

The **hamadryas** baboon lives in the rocky, open country or the desert. It is silver-colored with thick **ruffs** of fur around its shoulders. It does not have colors on its face.

Africa

Saudi Arabia

10

Mountain baboons have fur **ruffs**, but they also have heart-shaped patches of skin on their chests. Their head is rounded, and they have a large lower jaw. They are called **gelada** baboons.

The **savanna** baboons are named for the grasslands where they live. They are the most **common** baboon and live in many different countries in Africa. In one area, the animals are black-faced with olive green fur. In other **regions**, they are yellow, brown or olive-brown. Their tails are longer than the other **species** of baboons.

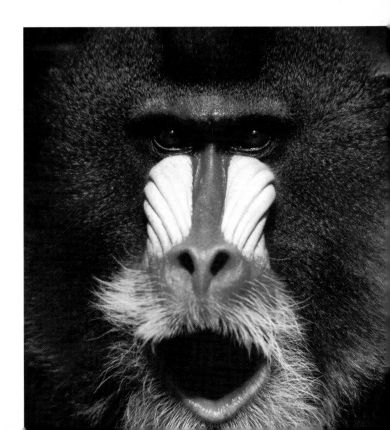

A mandrill baboon is very colorful.

The Baboon Troop

Baboons live in small family groups but they travel in **troops**. A troop can be as few as 10 animals or as many as 100 animals. The strongest and largest male baboon becomes the leader of the troop. All the monkeys will follow him when he goes to look for food. And when he stops to sleep, the rest of the troop sleeps too.

The baboons do not actually walk behind their leader. They **surround** him. The leader stays in the center of the pack with all the mothers and babies close beside him. The other baboons walk outside this circle so the babies will be protected on all sides. They watch for snakes or animals that might attack them. Any baboon who spots danger will make a shrill bark. Then the leader will leap out, ready to fight.

Each day, the monkeys will travel, feed, and rest side by side. Baboons in a troop will stay together all their lives.

A troop of baboons on a path in Kenya, Africa.

The Troop Leader

The leader of the **troop** must be **fierce** and brave to protect the baboons from larger animals. He is not afraid to fight lions, leopards, or wild dogs if they **threaten** any member of his troop. He will face his enemy and open his mouth to show off his large, sharp teeth. His fur bristles into a stiff collar around his face. He roars loudly. The leader looks so frightening that he rarely needs to fight. Often the bigger animal will run away from him.

The baboon leader must also control the members of his own troop when they fight each other. If he does attack another baboon, he will bite it on the back of the neck. The skin there is loose and protected by thick fur. The bite will not injure the other monkey.

Usually the leader can keep order just by staring into the eyes of the troublemaker. This is seen as a **threat**. Like many animals, baboons never look directly into each other's eyes when they are being friendly. To them, **eye contact** is a **challenge** or a **signal** that they are ready to attack.

This troop leader shows its fierce teeth.

Food

Baboons eat many things: fruit, vegetables, flowers, plants, grass, seeds, grains, bird eggs, honey, and insects. Sometimes they eat small animals such as lizards, mice, and snails.

Food is **scarce** on the **savanna** where most baboons live. A baboon **troop** spends most of the day hunting for food. This search may take them 12 miles away.

They are very clever and imaginative food gatherers. They turn over rocks to collect worms, snails, and insects. They know how to find termites in the bark of fallen trees. They can break open hard nutshells by hitting them with stones. They are even able to **thresh** wild wheat by pounding it against rocks until all the grain falls out.

Baboons use their fingers to scoop plant roots and seeds out of the ground. They roll their food on the grass or between their palms to soften it and to clean off any dirt. Sometimes they even wash their food.

Baboons like to eat flowers.

Babies

The birth of a baby is an exciting event in the baboon **troop**. The whole troop loves babies. They all want to hold and pet the little one.

A newborn infant has a pink face and sparse black hair over its body. It clings to the fur on its mother's stomach for the first few weeks. It will be able to walk when it is two weeks old.

At five weeks, it will begin to ride on its mother's back, like a jockey rides a horse. The mother baboon bends her back leg and lowers her body so the baby can climb up onto her back. Once the baby is settled, she will raise up her tail to brace against its back for support.

Baboon mothers are devoted and **fiercely** protective. When the baby strays away, its mother will pull it back to her by the tail.

Baboons, mother and young.

How They Grow

The baby learns by copying everything its mother does. It **imitates** the sounds she makes. It learns that lip smacks are a friendly greeting and that grunts and barks warn of danger. As they play, babies giggle just like human children.

Young baboons enjoy being with other animals. They like to chase each other or play with **chimpanzees**. The baby chimpanzees like different games. They would rather wrestle and roll on the ground than play chase.

Baboons are fascinated by little animals. They sometimes play with lizards or ducklings or baby monkeys. They may even keep them as pets.

After it is one year old, the baboon is able to be on its own, but it will stay with the same **troop**.

A young
baboon
hanging
from a
tree.

Glossary

affection - To show fondness or love.

apes - A group of primates, which includes gorillas, chimpanzees, orangutans, and gibbons.

challenge - (CHAL-ehnj) A dare or threat.

chimpanzees - A group of small, dark-haired apes from Africa.

common - Ordinary or widespread.

differs - To be unlike.

eye contact - Looking directly into the eyes of another.

fierce - (firs) Savage or cruel.

gelada - (juh-LAH-duh) A type of baboon with a round head and large jaw.

hamadryas - A type of baboon with a fur ruff around its shoulders found in Africa and Arabia.

imitates - Copies.

limbs - Arms or legs.

mandrill - A type of baboon with colorful markings.

muzzle - The mouth, nose, and jaw of an animal.

primates - (PRIE-maytz) A group of animals, which includes humans, apes, and monkeys.

region - (RE-jen) An area or place.

ruffs - Fringe or tufts of hair growing around the neck.

savanna - A region of flat, grassland.

scarce - Not common; hard to get.

signal - A sign.

social - Liking to be with others.

species - (SPEE-sheez) A group of animals that are alike in certain ways.

surround - To gather around an object; enclose.

threaten - To be dangerous.

thresh - To separate the grain from wheat.

troops - Groups.

Index